## XTREME WRESTLING ROYALTY
# JOHN CENA

A&D Xtreme
BOLD HI-LO NONFICTION

An imprint of Abdo Publishing
abdobooks.com

### ALEX MONNIG

## TAKE IT TO THE XTREME!

GET READY FOR AN EXTREME ADVENTURE! THE PAGES OF THIS BOOK WILL TAKE YOU INTO THE THRILLING WORLD OF PROFESSIONAL WRESTLING. WHEN YOU HAVE FINISHED READING THIS BOOK, TAKE THE XTREME CHALLENGE ON PAGE 45 ABOUT WHAT YOU'VE LEARNED!

ABDOBOOKS.COM

Published by Abdo Publishing, a division of ABDO, PO Box 398166, Minneapolis, Minnesota 55439. Copyright © 2024 by Abdo Consulting Group, Inc. International copyrights reserved in all countries. No part of this book may be reproduced in any form without written permission from the publisher. A&D Xtreme™ is a trademark and logo of Abdo Publishing.
Printed in the United States of America, North Mankato, MN.
052023
092023

THIS BOOK CONTAINS RECYCLED MATERIALS

Design: Kelly Doudna, Mighty Media, Inc.
Production: Mighty Media, Inc.
Editor: Katherine Chu
Cover Photograph: MediaPunch Master/AP Images
Interior Photographs: Alexander Vaughn/Wikimedia Commons, p. 23; anouchka/iStockphoto, pp. 12-13; Courtesy of Springfield College, Archives and Special Collections, pp. 10-11; Don Feria/AP Images, pp. 30-31; Ed Webster/Flickr, pp. 34-35; Ethan Miller/Getty Images, pp. 4-5; felipe bascuñan/Flickr, pp. 26-27; Franticpower/Wikimedia Commons, p. 22; JBZA2003/Wikimedia Commons, pp. 18-19; Jennifer Gasparovic, wish coordinator, Kids Wish Network/Wikimedia Commons, p. 43; John Phelan/Wikimedia Commons, pp. 8-9; Jonathan Bachman/AP Images, pp. 40-41, 44; lev radin/Shutterstock Images, p. 42; Megan Elice Meadows/Flickr, pp. 14-15, 36-37; Mel Evans/AP Images, pp. 28-29; Miguel Discart/Flickr, pp. 16-17, 20-21, 32-33; Ralph Dominguez/MediaPunch/AP Images, p. 9; Sam Aronov/Shutterstock Images, p. 1; WENN Rights Ltd/Alamy Photo, pp. 24-25; Wikimedia Commons, pp. 6-7, 38-39
Design Elements: amgun/Shutterstock Images (perspective); sanchesnet1/iStockphoto (spikes color, bolts); Wth/Shutterstock Images (stripes)

### LIBRARY OF CONGRESS CONTROL NUMBER: 2022948819
### PUBLISHER'S CATALOGING-IN-PUBLICATION DATA
Names: Monnig, Alex, author.
Title: John Cena / by Alex Monnig
Description: Minneapolis, Minnesota : Abdo Publishing, 2024 | Series: Xtreme wrestling royalty | Includes online resources and index.
Identifiers: ISBN 9781098291440 (lib. bdg.) | ISBN 9781098277901 (ebook)
Subjects: LCSH: Cena, John--Juvenile literature. | Wrestlers--Biography--Juvenile literature. | Actors--Biography--Juvenile literature. | World Wrestling Entertainment, Inc--Juvenile literature.
Classification: DDC 796.812092--dc23

# TABLE OF CONTENTS

DEFENDING THE CHAMPIONSHIP ........................ 4
A STRONG START ......................................... 6
THE ULTIMATE LIFE-CHANGING DECISION ......... 12
RISING STAR OF WRESTLING .......................... 16
MAKING A NAME FOR HIMSELF ...................... 22
BECOMING A SUPERSTAR .............................. 28
ADORING FANS AND RUTHLESS RIVALS ............ 32
MEMORABLE MOVES .................................... 36
OUTSIDE THE RING ...................................... 38
INSPIRING CHAMPION .................................. 44
XTREME CHALLENGE .................................... 45
GLOSSARY .................................................. 46
ONLINE RESOURCES .................................... 47
INDEX ....................................................... 48

## CHAPTER 1
# DEFENDING THE CHAMPIONSHIP

In 2009, John Cena battled Randy "the **Legend** Killer" Orton. This was an hour-long, Anything Goes Iron Man Match.

Both wrestlers performed shocking **stunts**. Cena endured being hit with a TV monitor. And he narrowly avoided fireworks Orton used as a weapon! In the end, Cena won the match. The World Wrestling Entertainment (WWE) World Heavyweight Championship was his once again.

John Cena picks up Randy Orton during a WWE Raw match in 2009.

## CHAPTER 2
# A STRONG START

John Felix Anthony Cena Jr. was born on April 23, 1977, in West Newbury, Massachusetts. As an adult, John was very strong and powerful. But it took him years to become that way. John's interest in becoming strong started because his classmates picked on him at school.

John's father was a professional wrestling fan. Growing up, John often watched professional wrestling with his father on cable TV.

Beginning in his preteen years, John loved rap music and the hip-hop clothing style. This affected how he acted and dressed. John stood out from other kids. And they bullied him for this. To stop them, John decided to get bigger. He asked his father to buy him some weights. As John gained muscle, the bullying stopped.

John's love of rap music continued as he attended Central Catholic High School in Lawrence, Massachusetts, and into adulthood. In 2002, he dressed up as rapper Vanilla Ice (*pictured*), during a Halloween-themed episode of *SmackDown*.

Cena's interest in strength training carried into his time at Springfield College in Massachusetts. There, he studied **physiology**. After graduating in 1999, Cena moved to Los Angeles, California, and looked for work in the fitness industry. Little did he know where this path would lead him.

Cena (*left*) was a Springfield College football tri-captain along with Kevin Jordan (*center*) and Mike Fanning (*right*).

### XTREME FACT

Cena played football at Springfield College from 1996 to 1999. He played center and was a team captain from 1998 to 1999.

# CHAPTER 3
# THE ULTIMATE LIFE-CHANGING DECISION

After moving to Los Angeles, Cena started working at Gold's Gym. He also joined **bodybuilder** contests. In 2000, a friend invited Cena to train with Ultimate Pro Wrestling (UPW) at the Ultimate University wrestling center. The invitation changed his life forever.

The Gold's Gym where Cena worked was a popular training spot for bodybuilders.

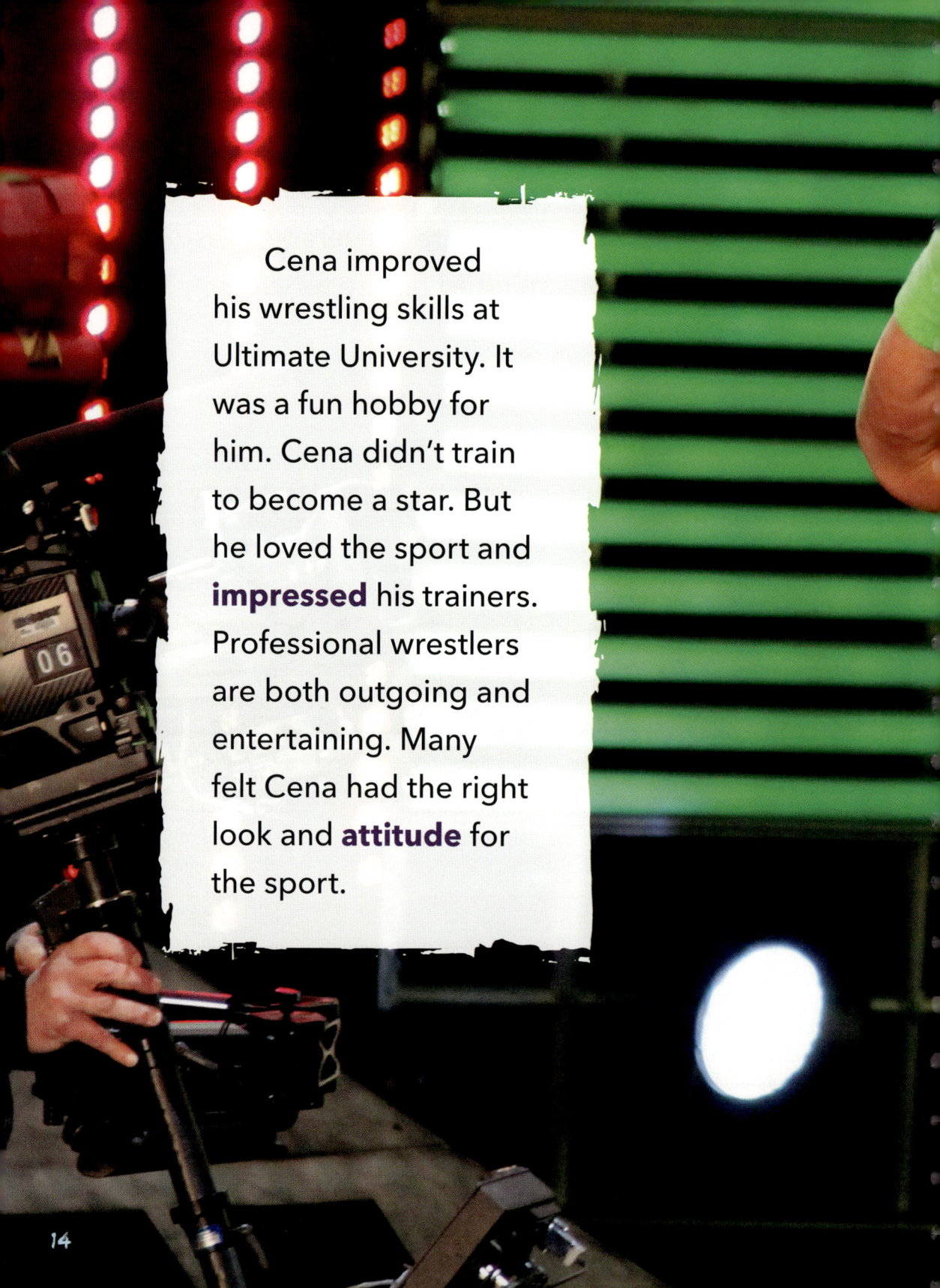

Cena improved his wrestling skills at Ultimate University. It was a fun hobby for him. Cena didn't train to become a star. But he loved the sport and **impressed** his trainers. Professional wrestlers are both outgoing and entertaining. Many felt Cena had the right look and **attitude** for the sport.

**Cena salutes his fans before entering the ring. His salute is also a sign of respect to the men and women in the armed forces.**

# CHAPTER 4
# RISING STAR OF WRESTLING

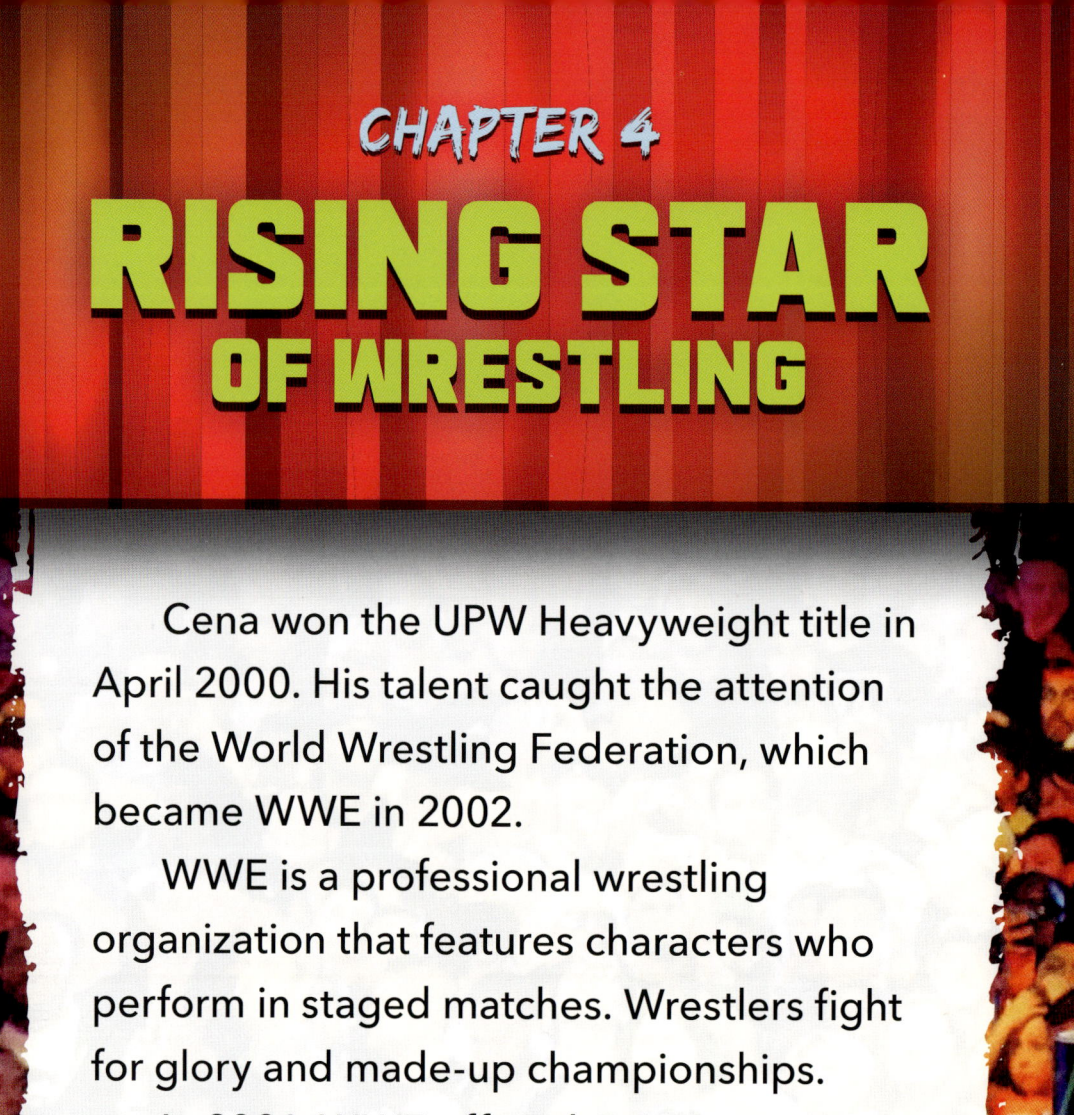

Cena won the UPW Heavyweight title in April 2000. His talent caught the attention of the World Wrestling Federation, which became WWE in 2002.

WWE is a professional wrestling organization that features characters who perform in staged matches. Wrestlers fight for glory and made-up championships.

In 2001, WWE offered Cena a contract to train in the Ohio Valley Wrestling (OVW) program. He won the OVW Heavyweight Championship in early 2002.

Cena's popularity has continued to rise since joining WWE. Many consider him to be a living legend.

In June 2002, Cena made his first WWE appearance on *SmackDown*. He answered an open challenge from Kurt Angle. Cena immediately attacked Angle with **ruthless aggression**. But Angle pinned Cena, ending the fight.

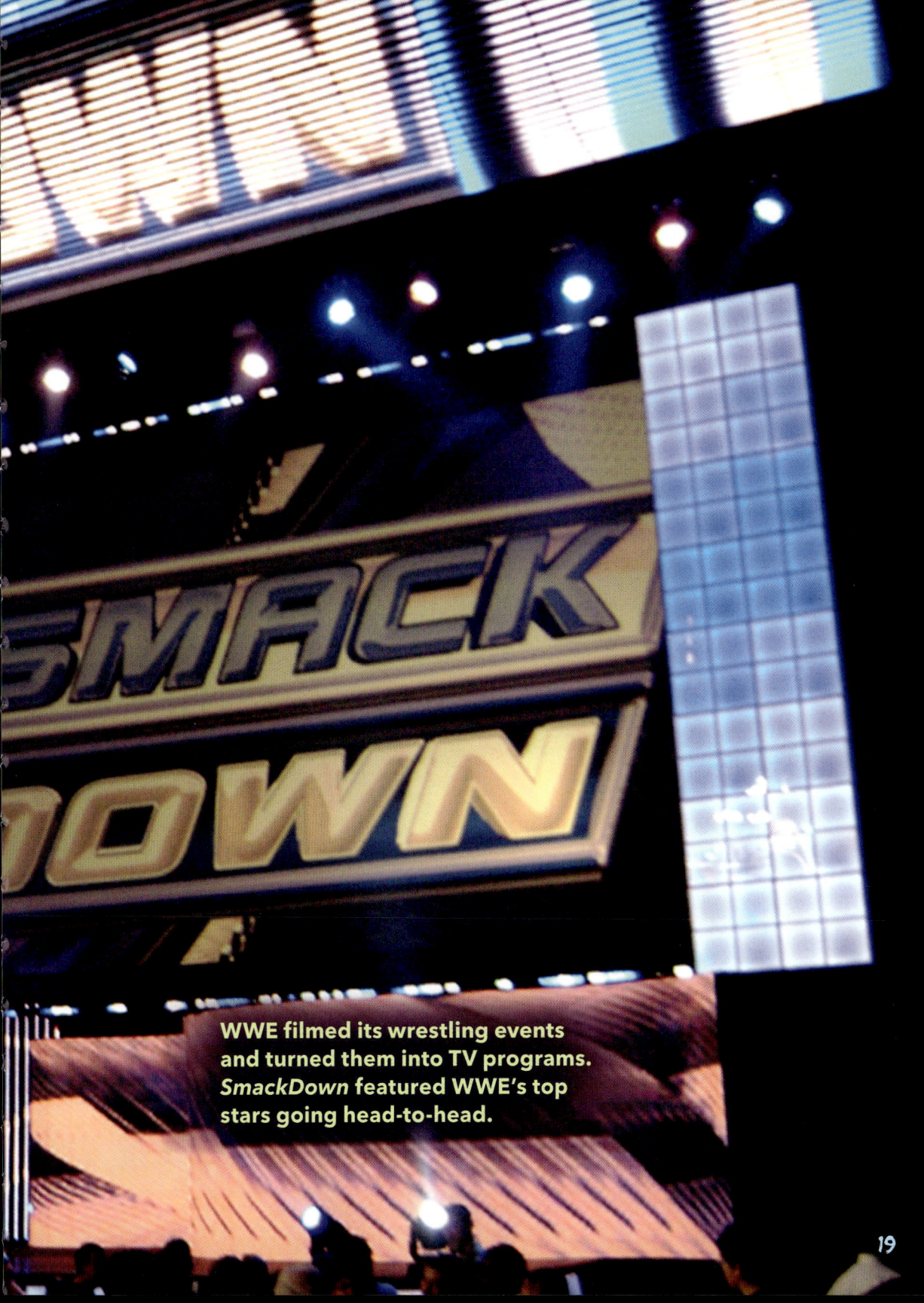

WWE filmed its wrestling events and turned them into TV programs. *SmackDown* featured WWE's top stars going head-to-head.

### XTREME FACT

Cena collects cars. He bought a 1989 Jeep Wrangler with his first WWE paycheck. He even made a video series called *John Cena: Auto Geek*.

Cena holding the United States Championship belt after winning a fight against Dean Ambrose in 2015

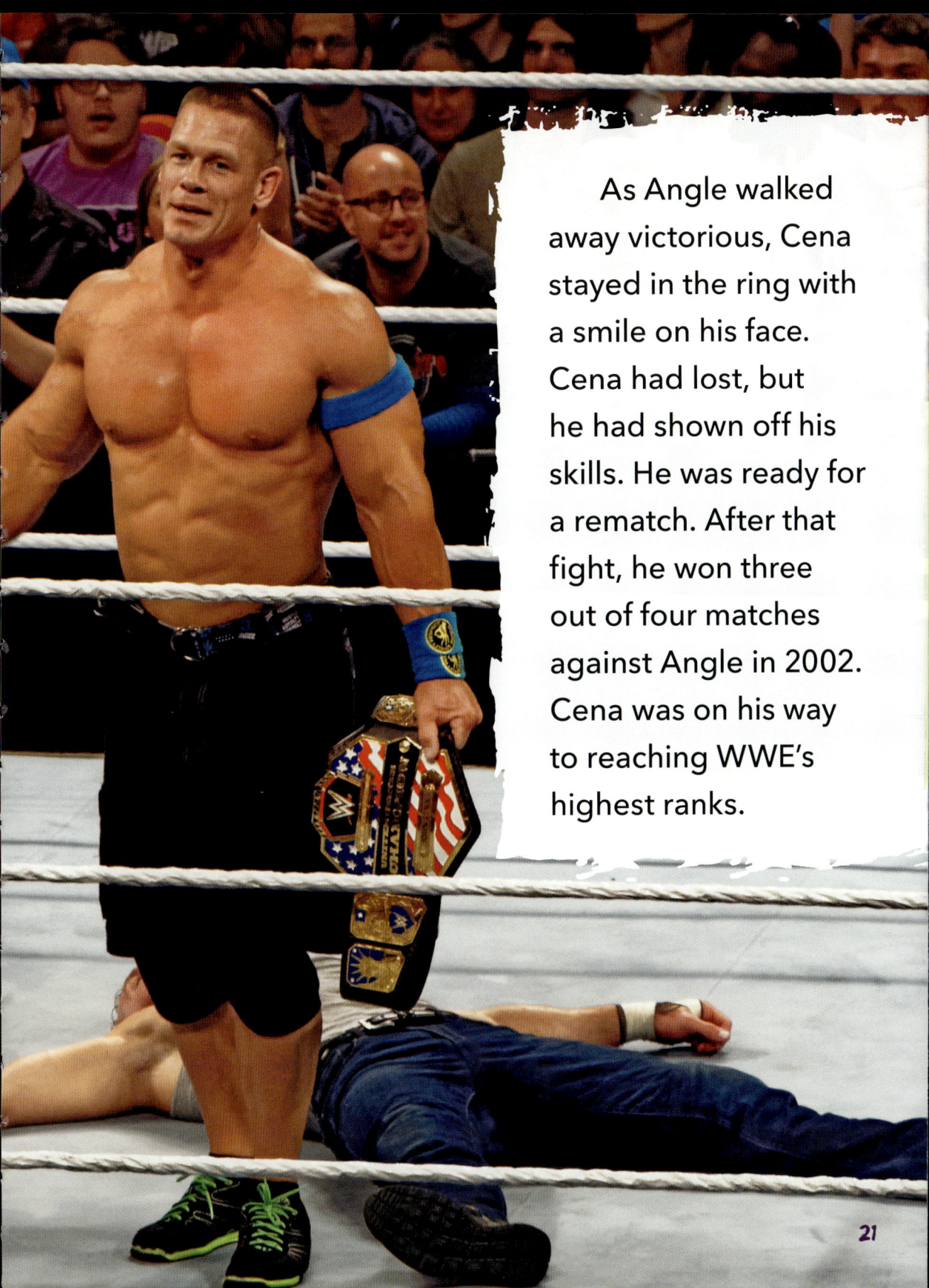

As Angle walked away victorious, Cena stayed in the ring with a smile on his face. Cena had lost, but he had shown off his skills. He was ready for a rematch. After that fight, he won three out of four matches against Angle in 2002. Cena was on his way to reaching WWE's highest ranks.

# Chapter 5
# Making a Name for Himself

Cena was a good fighter, but at first WWE leaders didn't think he was popular enough to keep. This changed when Cena **impressed** WWE management by **freestyle rapping** during a wrestling tour. WWE named him the Doctor of Thuganomics and let him rap before matches. Cena also wore backward hats, gold chains, and other clothing common in hip-hop style. The fashion choices that got him bullied as a child now saved his career! They also set him apart as a rising WWE star.

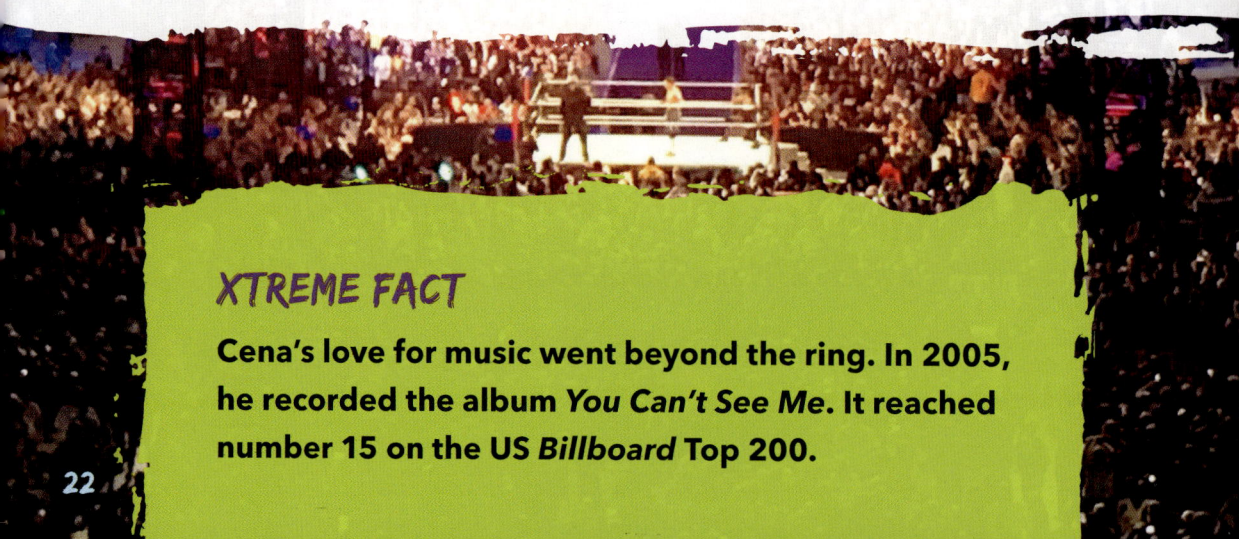

### XTREME FACT

Cena's love for music went beyond the ring. In 2005, he recorded the album *You Can't See Me*. It reached number 15 on the US *Billboard* Top 200.

Cena performing in front of the crowd before a match

In 2009, Cena defeated the Big Show (*center*) again during a WWE Raw match.

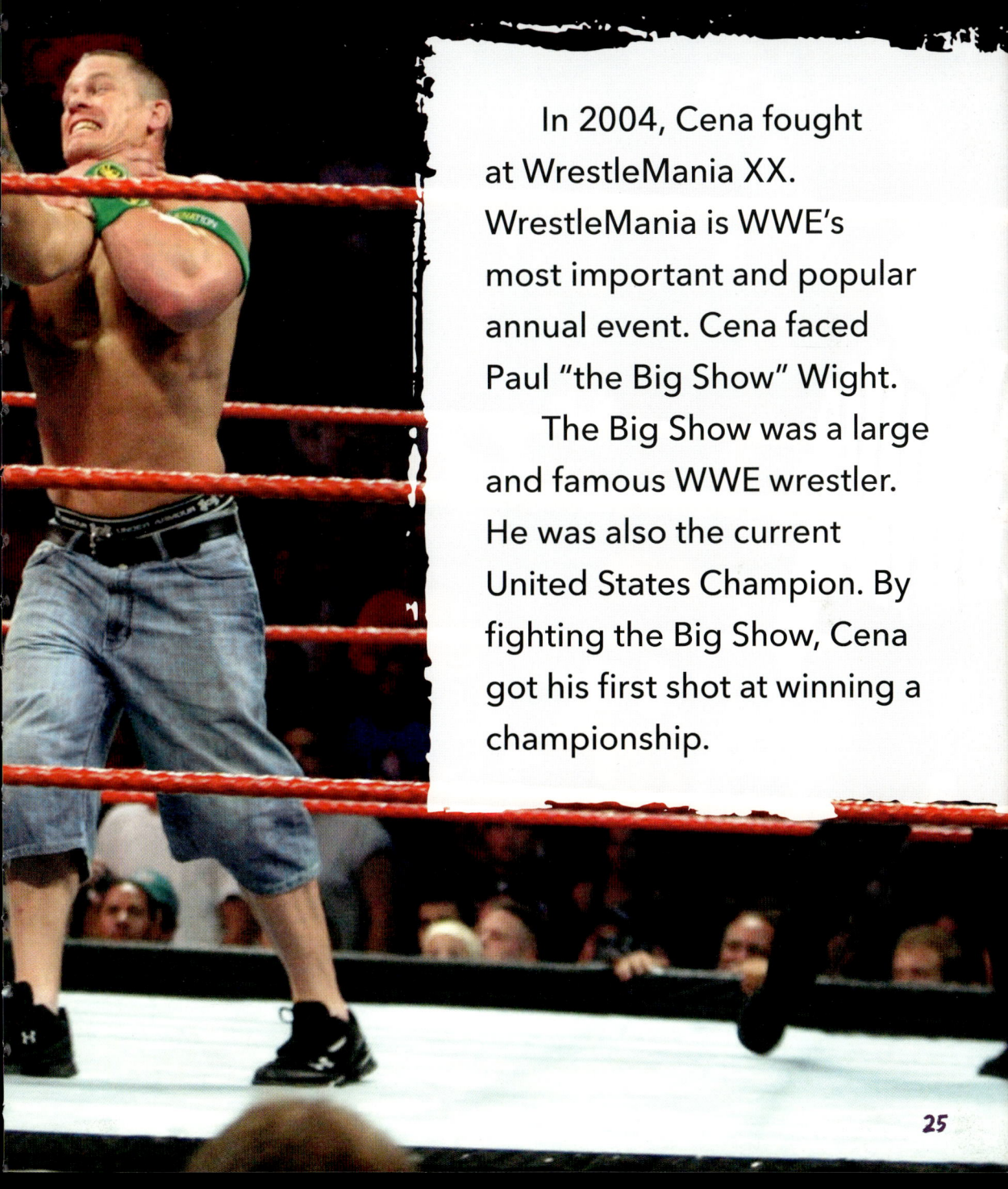

In 2004, Cena fought at WrestleMania XX. WrestleMania is WWE's most important and popular annual event. Cena faced Paul "the Big Show" Wight.

The Big Show was a large and famous WWE wrestler. He was also the current United States Champion. By fighting the Big Show, Cena got his first shot at winning a championship.

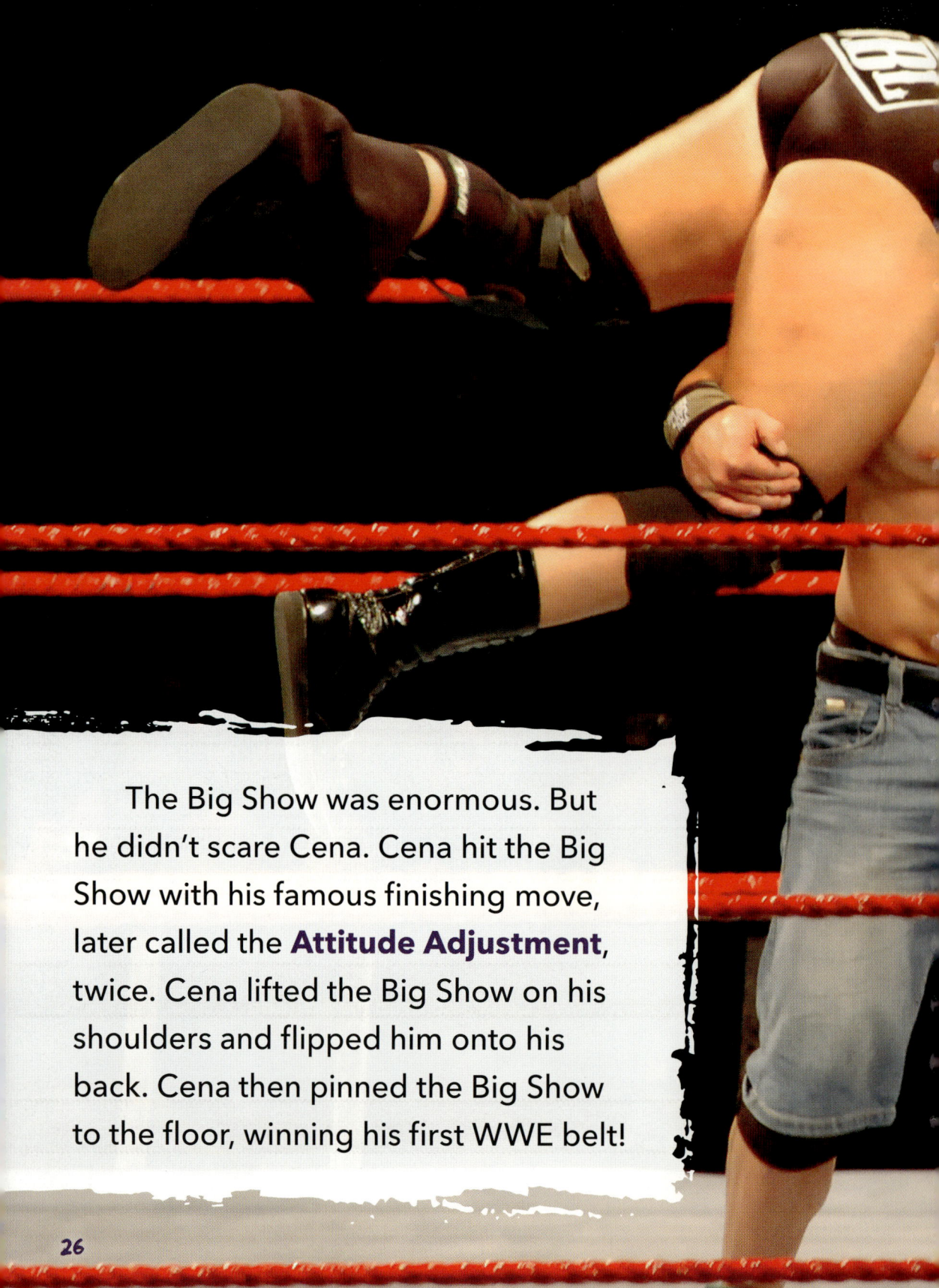

The Big Show was enormous. But he didn't scare Cena. Cena hit the Big Show with his famous finishing move, later called the **Attitude Adjustment**, twice. Cena lifted the Big Show on his shoulders and flipped him onto his back. Cena then pinned the Big Show to the floor, winning his first WWE belt!

Cena also used his Attitude Adjustment move on John Layfield during a WWE Raw match in 2008.

# CHAPTER 6
# BECOMING A SUPERSTAR

Cena won his first WWE World Heavyweight Championship at WrestleMania XXII in 2006. He held the title on and off for the next two and a half years. Whenever he lost the championship to a rival, he would win it back during their next match.

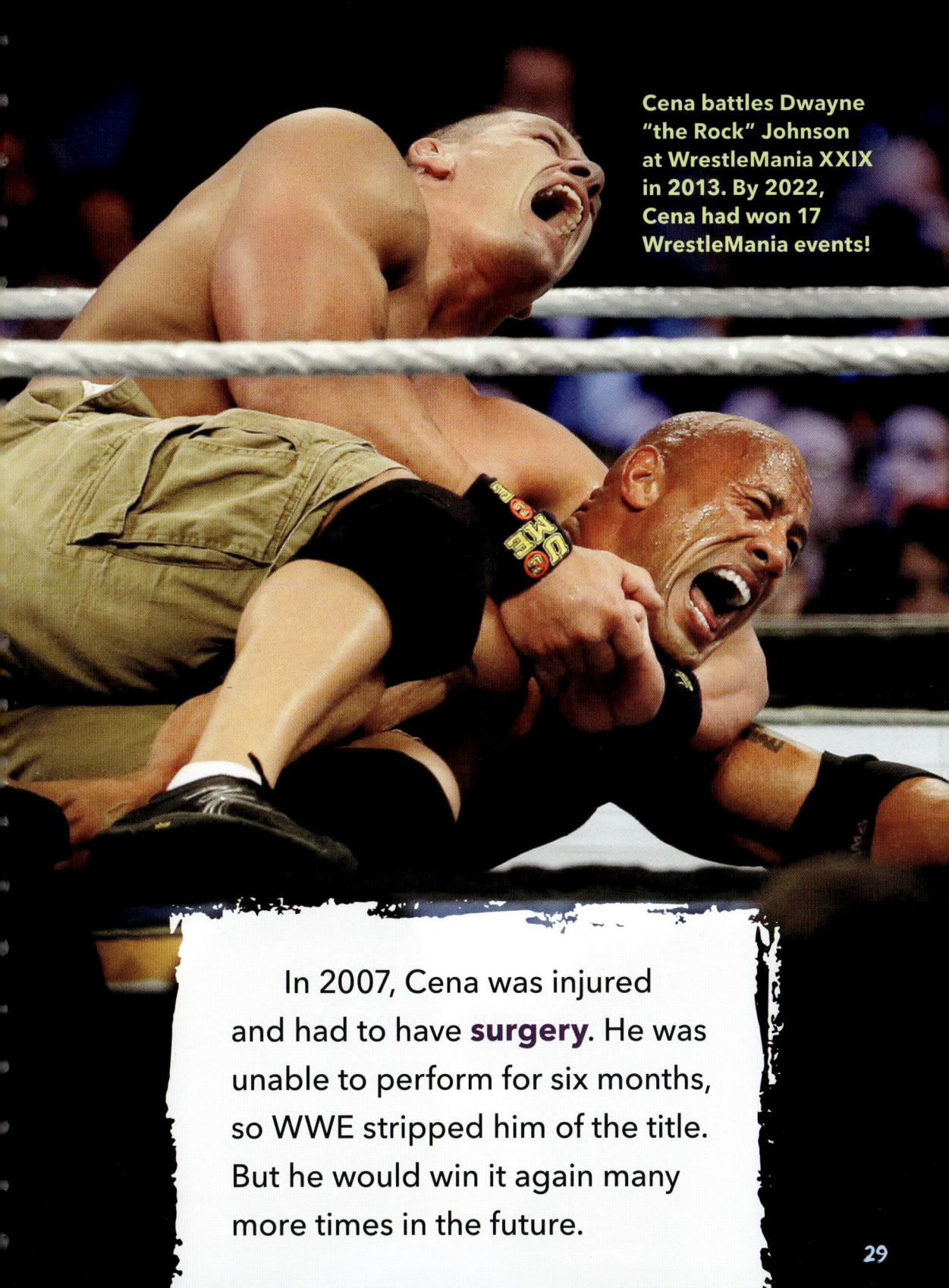

Cena battles Dwayne "the Rock" Johnson at WrestleMania XXIX in 2013. By 2022, Cena had won 17 WrestleMania events!

In 2007, Cena was injured and had to have **surgery**. He was unable to perform for six months, so WWE stripped him of the title. But he would win it again many more times in the future.

### XTREME FACT

**Cena shares the record of 16 WWE World Heavyweight Championship wins with wrestler Ric Flair.**

Over the next 10 years, Cena earned the title of WWE World Heavyweight Champion a record 16 times! After his sixteenth win in 2017, WWE made him the face of the organization. He was now the most popular WWE wrestler and its top star.

Cena using his Stepover Toehold Facelock move on Rusev Barnyashev during a WWE SmackDown event in 2015

# CHAPTER 7
# ADORING FANS
## AND RUTHLESS RIVALS

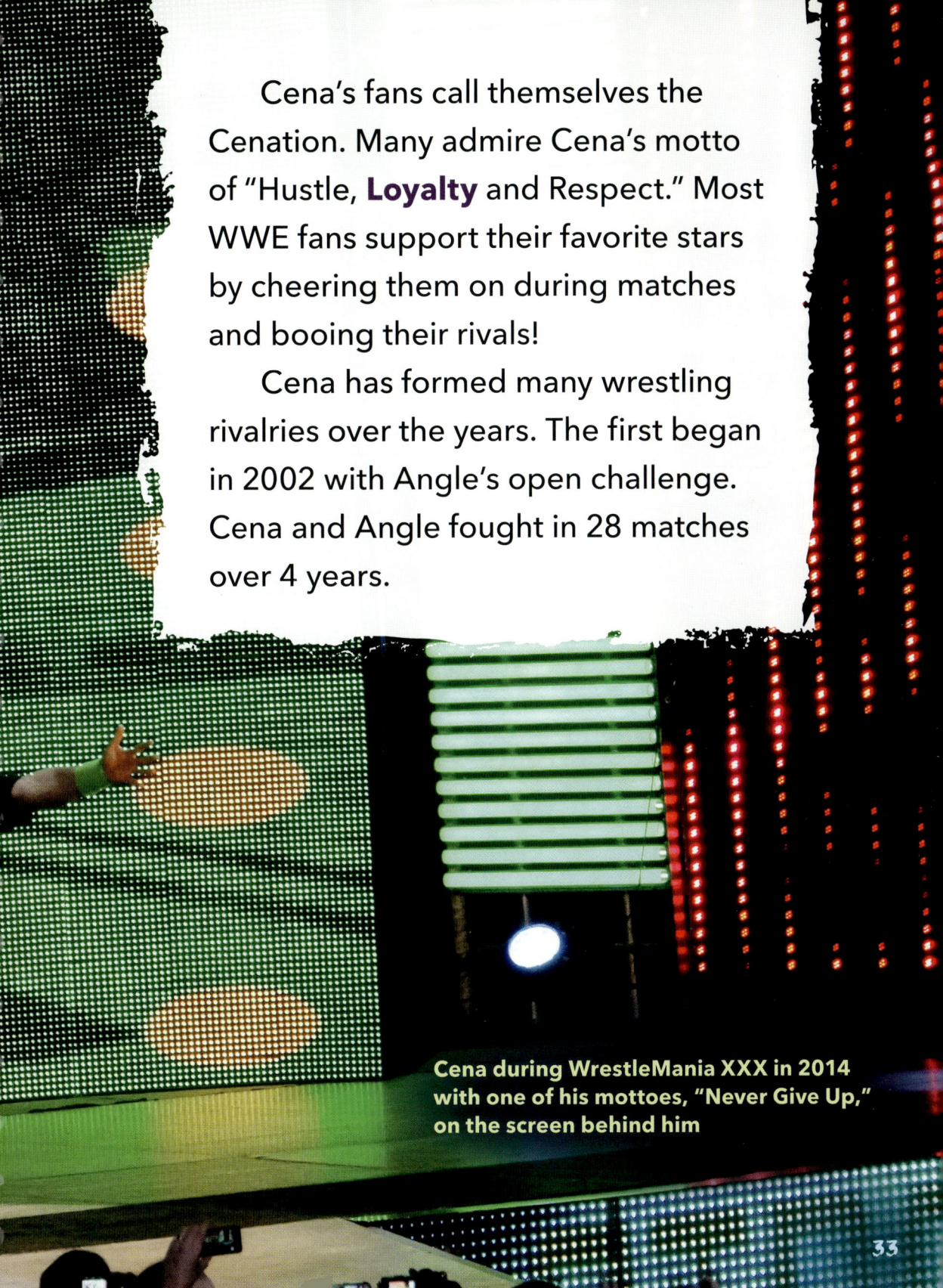

Cena's fans call themselves the Cenation. Many admire Cena's motto of "Hustle, **Loyalty** and Respect." Most WWE fans support their favorite stars by cheering them on during matches and booing their rivals!

Cena has formed many wrestling rivalries over the years. The first began in 2002 with Angle's open challenge. Cena and Angle fought in 28 matches over 4 years.

Cena during WrestleMania XXX in 2014 with one of his mottoes, "Never Give Up," on the screen behind him

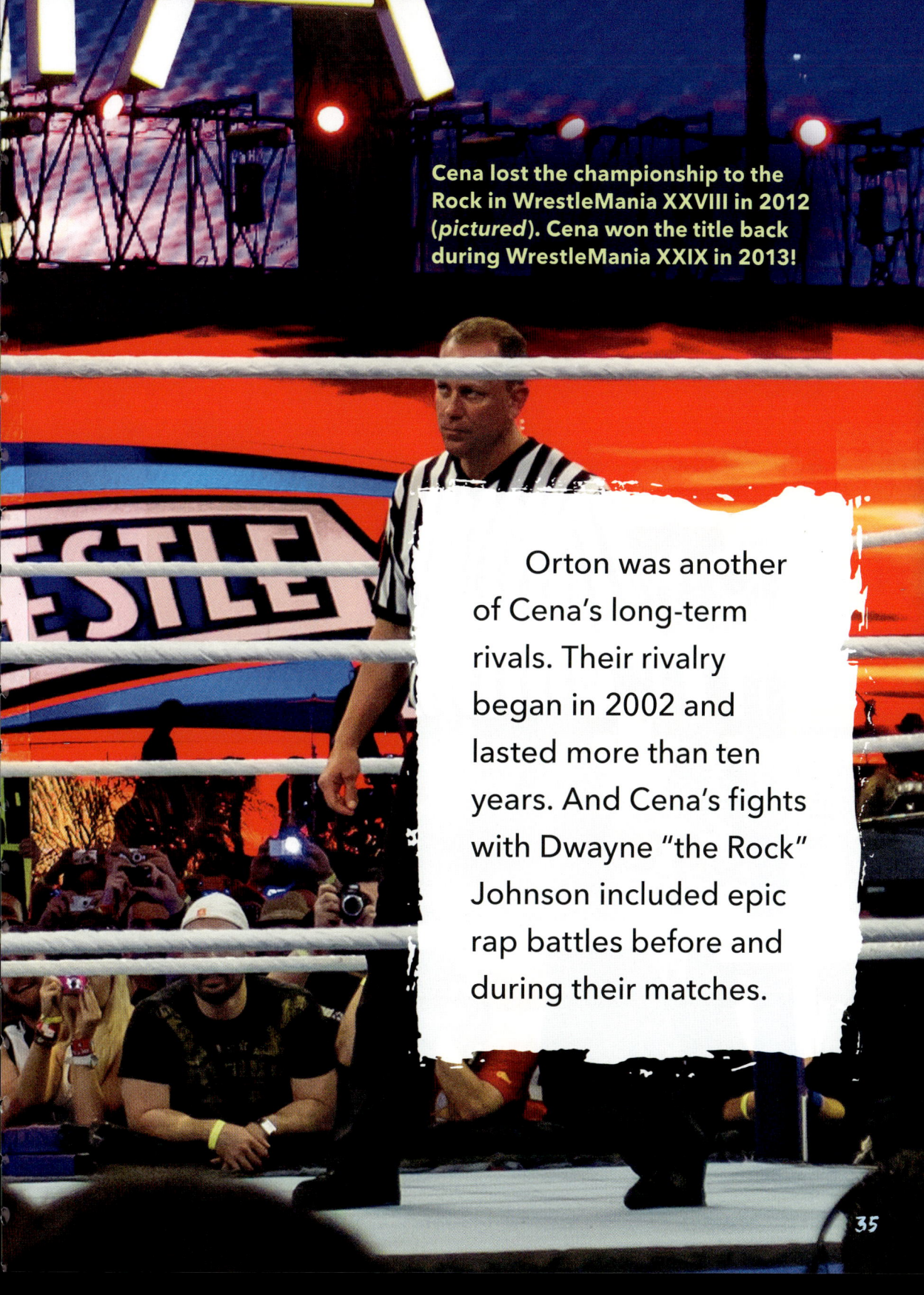

Cena lost the championship to the Rock in WrestleMania XXVIII in 2012 (*pictured*). Cena won the title back during WrestleMania XXIX in 2013!

Orton was another of Cena's long-term rivals. Their rivalry began in 2002 and lasted more than ten years. And Cena's fights with Dwayne "the Rock" Johnson included epic rap battles before and during their matches.

# CHAPTER 8
# MEMORABLE MOVES

Cena used a chair against Erick Rowan during WrestleMania XXX in 2014.

Cena has a few famous wrestling moves. One is his finishing move, the **Attitude Adjustment**. Cena is also known for a move that includes one of his famous sayings. He waves a hand in front of his face and says, "You can't see me." He then performs a jumping punch to his opponent's head.

### XTREME FACT

**Cena first used his Stepover Toehold Facelock move in 2005. It was based on Angle's famous ankle lock.**

## CHAPTER 9
# OUTSIDE THE RING

Cena has become well known outside of WWE too. In 2006, he made his first movie appearance, starring in *The Marine*. Since then, Cena has appeared in many movies and TV shows. He's played a dad, a superhero, and a military officer. He even voiced the cartoon character Ferdinand the bull in the 2017 film *Ferdinand*.

Cena played the character John Triton in *The Marine*.

Cena celebrates his win at WrestleMania XXX in 2014.

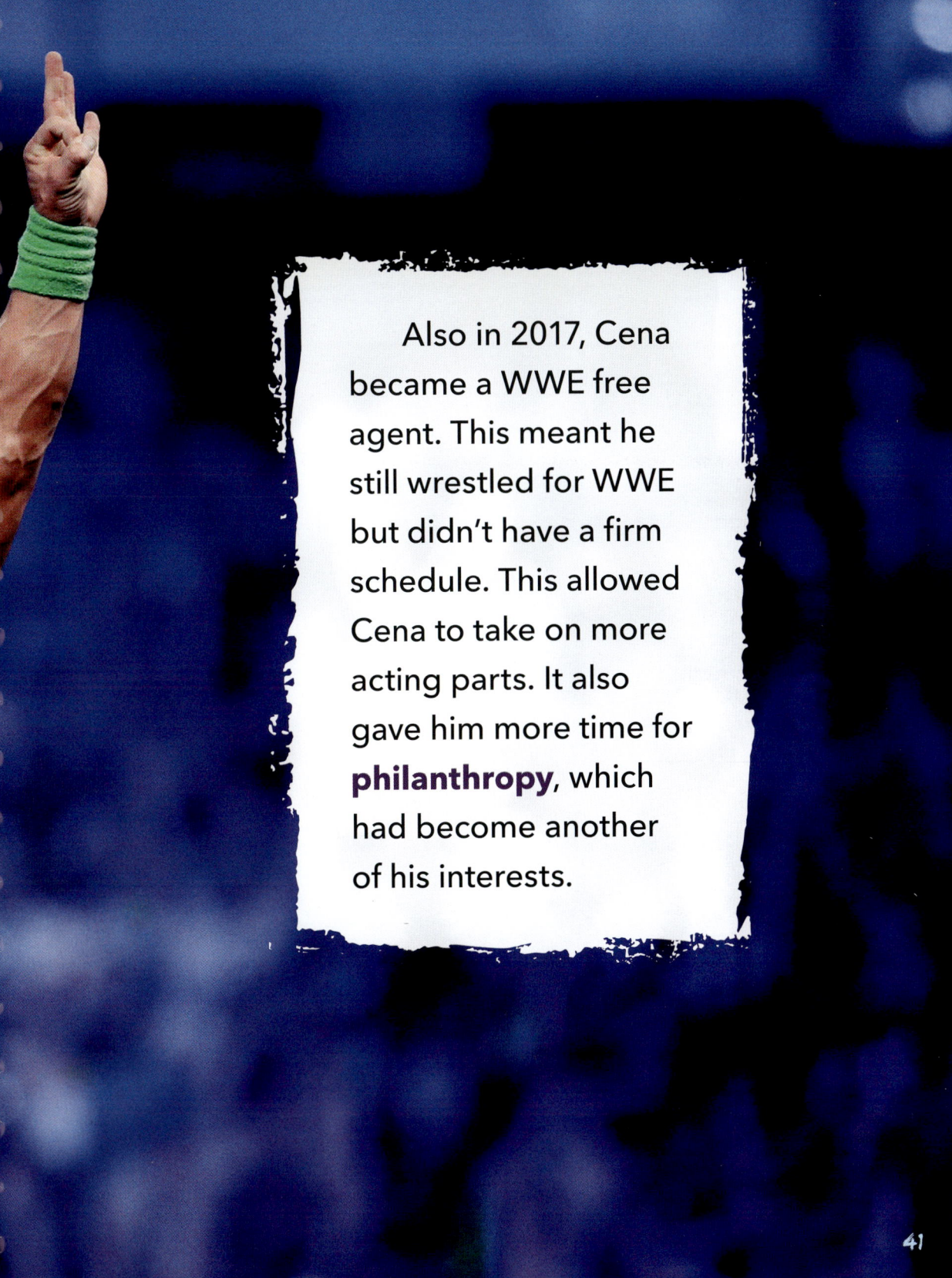

Also in 2017, Cena became a WWE free agent. This meant he still wrestled for WWE but didn't have a firm schedule. This allowed Cena to take on more acting parts. It also gave him more time for **philanthropy**, which had become another of his interests.

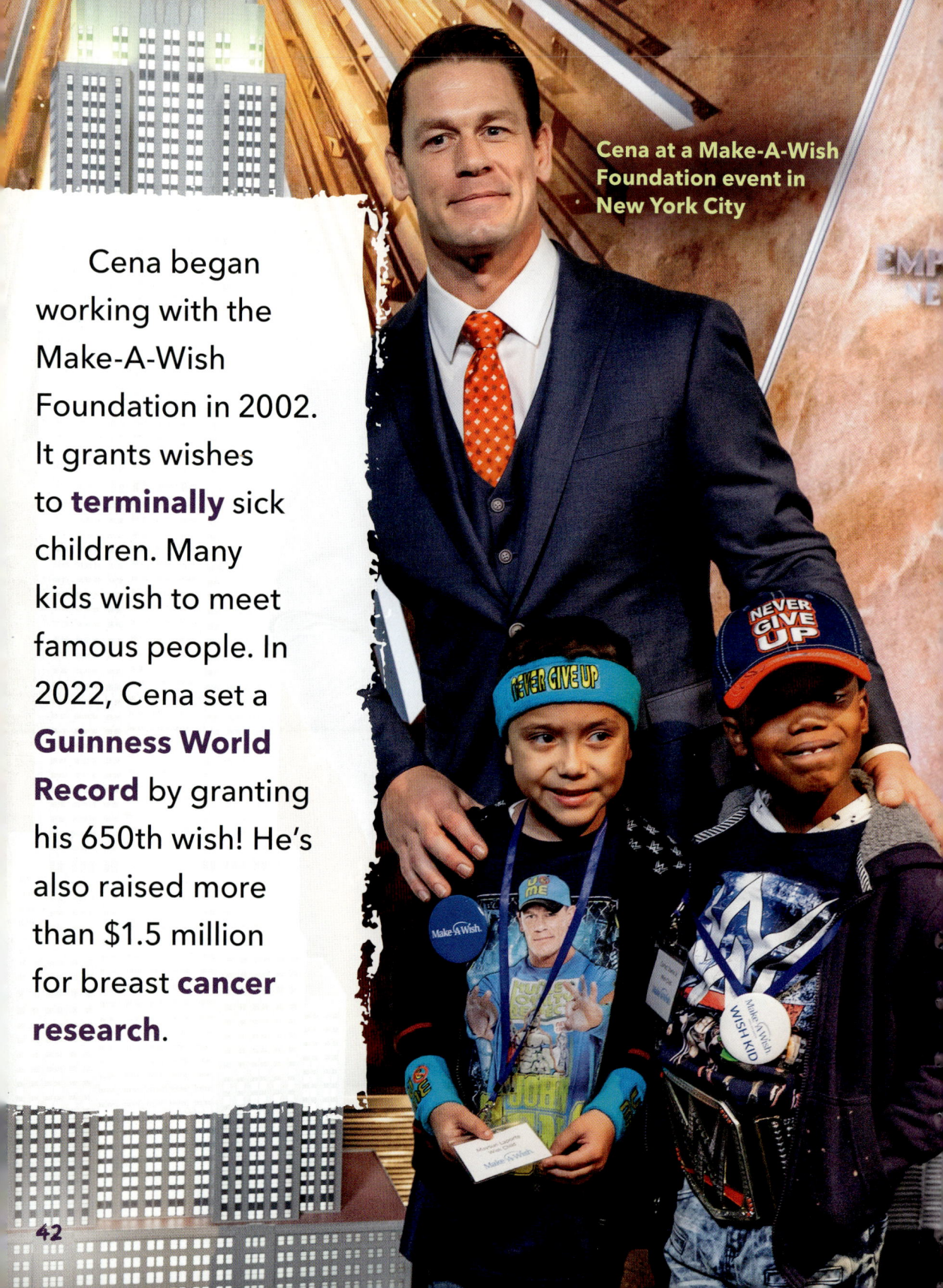

Cena at a Make-A-Wish Foundation event in New York City

Cena began working with the Make-A-Wish Foundation in 2002. It grants wishes to **terminally** sick children. Many kids wish to meet famous people. In 2022, Cena set a **Guinness World Record** by granting his 650th wish! He's also raised more than $1.5 million for breast **cancer research**.

In 2019, the Make-A-Wish Foundation stated that Cena was children's most-requested celebrity to meet. It said this is because Cena promotes strength, hope, and transformation.

# CHAPTER 10
# INSPIRING CHAMPION

Cena has built a successful career outside wrestling. But he isn't ready to give up his spot in the ring yet! He is a WWE star who encourages others to be respectful and **loyal**. To his fans, Cena will forever be wrestling royalty.

# XTREME CHALLENGE

### TAKE THE QUIZ BELOW AND PUT WHAT YOU'VE LEARNED TO THE TEST!

1) Which wrestler's open challenge did John Cena answer during his WWE debut in 2002?

2) What would your wrestling character be known for if you joined WWE?

3) While at Springfield College, what sport did Cena play?

4) Which personality traits do you think helped Cena achieve success in wrestling?

5) What type of music did Cena love as a preteen?

# GLOSSARY

**adjustment**—the act of changing or conforming.

**aggression**—hostile or violent behavior.

**attitude**—the way you think or feel about something.

**bodybuilder**—a person who develops their body through exercise and diet.

**cancer**—any of a group of very harmful diseases that cause a body's cells to become unhealthy.

**freestyle rap**—a style of rap in which lyrics are recited with no particular structure and no preparation.

**Guinness World Record**—a published list of world records for human achievements.

**impress**—to cause someone to feel admiration or respect.

**legend**—a famous or important person, place, or thing that is known for doing something very well.

**loyal**—faithful or devoted to someone or something. The quality or state of being loyal is called loyalty.

**philanthropy**—doing things to help make life better for other people.

**physiology**—the branch of biology that deals with the normal functions of living organisms and their parts.

**research**—careful study of a subject to learn facts about it.

**ruthless**—having or showing no compassion for others.

**stunt**—an unusual or daring action used to gain attention.

**surgery**—the treating of sickness or injury by cutting into and repairing body parts.

**terminal**—predicted to lead to death.

# ONLINE RESOURCES

To learn more about John Cena, please visit **abdobooklinks.com** or scan this QR code. These links are routinely monitored and updated to provide the most current information available.

# INDEX

**A**
acting, 38, 41
Angle, Kurt, 18, 21, 33, 37
ankle lock, 37
Anything Goes Iron Man Match, 4
Attitude Adjustment, 26, 37

**B**
bodybuilding, 13
breast cancer research, 42

**C**
cars, 20
Cenation, 33
championships
   OVW Heavyweight, 16
   UPW Heavyweight, 16
   WWE United States, 25, 26
   WWE World Heavyweight, 4, 28, 29, 30, 31

**D**
"Doctor of Thuganomics," 22

**F**
famous sayings, 37
*Ferdinand*, 38
Flair, Ric, 30
football, 11
free agent, 41

**G**
Gold's Gym, 13
Guinness World Record, 42

**J**
Jeep Wrangler, 20
*John Cena: Auto Geek*, 20
Johnson, Dwayne "the Rock," 35

**M**
Make-A-Wish Foundation, 42
*Marine, The*, 38
motto, 33
music, 8, 22, 35

**O**
Ohio Valley Wrestling (OVW), 17
Orton, Randy, 4, 35

**P**
philanthropy, 41, 42

**S**
*SmackDown*, 18
Springfield College, 10, 11
Stepover Toehold Facelock, 37

strength training, 6, 8, 10, 13
surgery, 29

**U**
Ultimate Pro Wrestling (UPW), 13, 16
Ultimate University wrestling center, 13, 14

**W**
West Newbury, Massachusetts, 6
Wight, Paul "the Big Show," 25, 26
World Wrestling Entertainment (WWE), 4, 16, 18, 20, 21, 22, 25, 26, 28, 29, 30, 31, 33, 38, 41, 44
World Wrestling Federation, 16
WrestleMania
   XX, 25
   XXII, 28

**Y**
*You Can't See Me*, 22